PORNOGRAPHY:
THE POLLUTING OF AMERICA

LIFE'S ANSWER SERIES

James Robison

PORNO-GRAPHY
THE POLLUTING OF AMERICA

TYNDALE HOUSE
PUBLISHERS, INC.
WHEATON, ILLINOIS

All Scripture references are taken from the
King James Version of the Bible, unless otherwise noted.

First Printing, February 1982

Library of Congress Catalog Card Number 81-84600
ISBN 0-8423-4858-1
Printed in the United States of America

CONTENTS

INTRODUCTION

A friend of mine who served on the staff of a daily newspaper wrote an editorial advocating laws to restrict the spread of pornographic peep shows, movie houses, and magazine stands in his community. The day after the editorial appeared a young reporter for the newspaper burst into my friend's office in a near rage. He proceeded to lambaste the Christian editorial writer for promoting "censorship" and to inform him that pornography represented no threat to the community. "There's not one shred of evidence that pornographic material affects behavior in any harmful way," the young man protested.

Is pornography a problem? Or is it just a harmless fad that will soon run its polluted course and fade away?

I believe the answer to those questions is self-evident to anyone familiar with the Word of God and sensitive to the teaching of the Holy Spirit.

While the Scriptures contain no direct references to pornography, they are filled with proclamations and instructions whose import speaks volumes against such filth. For example, the Bible warns repeatedly against the things that corrupt people.

"Take ye therefore good heed unto yourselves. . . . Lest ye corrupt yourselves. . . " (Deut. 4:15,16).

"Be not deceived: evil communications corrupt good manners [or good behavior]" (1 Cor. 15:33).

"Let no corrupt communication proceed out of

your mouth, but that which is good to the use of edifying [building up]" (Eph. 4:29).

One passage of Scripture seems especially aimed at the pornographer:

"Likewise also these filthy dreamers defile the flesh, despise dominion, and speak evil of dignities. . . . [They] speak evil of those things which they know not: but what they know naturally, as brute beasts, in those things they corrupt themselves" (Jude 8, 10).

The dictionary definitions of the verb "to corrupt" help us see how the biblical injunctions against corruption apply to pornography.

To corrupt means "to change from a sound condition to an unsound one; to spoil, contaminate; to cause to rot."

Modern America and other countries that are aswim in pornography offer mounds of evidence that the traffic in filth works all of these debilitating effects on human society. I believe it is an instrument of Satan to change man's relationship to God and his fellow man, to spoil the union of husband and wife established by God as the foundation of society, and to contaminate the biblical concept of man as a creation of God and a being with individual worth and dignity.

Pornography is more than just an instrument of evil. It is an evidence of a deeper evil. It is not simply a problem in its own right, but the symptom of a more profound problem.

It is my prayer that this book may help concerned Christians become aware of the nature, scope, and danger of the pornography problem and motivate them to take action against it, in the wisdom and power of God.

ONE

IS PORNOGRAPHY A PROBLEM?

In May 1977 a modeling agency sent a young woman to a sporting goods store in New York City to audition as a model for an advertisement. A beautiful blonde, the model had attained remarkable success in her career for one so young. She was only nineteen, yet she was modeling for one of New York's top agencies. Her picture had appeared on the covers of national magazines.

When the model arrived at the sporting goods store, one of the owners drove her to the apartment of another man where he said the ad would be filmed. There the young woman soon learned to her horror that she had been taken to the apartment under false pretenses.

Three other men were waiting in the apartment, and, instead of filming an advertisement, they threatened the model's life, slapped her, and beat her repeatedly in an effort to force her to perform sexual acts for a video camera. When she refused to submit voluntarily, the men forced her to take drugs, then raped and sodomized her for several hours while the degrading activities were videotaped.

That sordid incident is only one of many that illustrate the insidious and corrupting effects of pornography.

God created man in his own image (Gen. 1:26, 27). This imbues man with an importance infinitely greater than that of animals and material things, as valuable as those may be. Other Scriptures picture a noble purpose as well as a noble status for man in God's scheme of things. He meant for man to perform fruitful work and to have communion with God and with his fellow man.

When Adam and Eve sinned, they broke their fellowship with God and profaned their purpose. In his redemptive work through Jesus Christ, however, God restores the fellowship between himself and man and re-equips men for the purpose he wants them to fulfill.

"That which we have seen and heard declare we unto you, that ye also may have fellowship with us: and truly our fellowship is with the Father, and with his Son Jesus Christ" (1 John 1:3).

"For we are his [God's] workmanship, created in Christ Jesus unto good works, which God hath before ordained [prepared] that we should walk in them" (Eph. 2:10).

Pornography works to destroy fellowship between God and man and between man and man. It acts to divert man from the "good works" that God ordained for him to do. It robs man of the worth and dignity God intended for him to know and feel when he created him in his own image.

The news story about the kidnapping and rape of the New York model gives a hideous illustration of how pornography functions to thwart God's will for men and women. It shows clearly what pornography teaches: That human beings are mere animals or, worse, that they are mere objects existing only to be used and exploited by other animals. With pornography, the highest value is sensual pleasure. Other people may be used to provide that pleasure and then discarded by the user.

God created sex. He made them "male and

female" (Gen. 1:27). In his grand design, though, sex was to be a means of expressing love, one of the many ways by which a man and woman would achieve the oneness God intended them to have in marriage (Gen. 2:24).

Pornography makes sex a dirty word. It destroys the purpose God intended sex to fulfill. It debases sex. To the man, it makes sex nothing but a biological urge that cries for satisfaction at any cost. The woman is presented as a mechanical device to be used in whatever way seems most likely to produce the desired satisfaction. She becomes just a robot, a toy for a moment's pleasure.

Some pornographers boast that their filthy representations are "telling it like it is" about sex. That's a lie. Pornography is not telling the truth about sex. Sex is an extremely intimate, private, and noble expression of love. Pornography pictures it as a coarse, demeaning act of exploitation. It cheats men and women of their God-given dignity. It depicts them as trash.

Through his redemptive work, God is striving to educate people in the principles of eternal life. God's values have been widely adopted in the educational processes that have produced civilized societies. By attacking these processes, pornography strikes at the very foundations of civilization.

William A. Stanmeyer, a constitutional lawyer, wrote about this aspect of the pornography problem several years ago in *The National Observer*. He said:

> Civilized society cannot afford to be neutral toward such a perception of life. For education to civility is an effort to make of man something more than a creature of elemental passions and

sensations. To civilize is to help people internalize respect for others, sharpen their sense of reality, grasp the difference between the decent and the indecent, desire the noble and eschew the ignoble, control their passions, do what is right even when it costs, stand in awe and wonder at such ultimate mysteries as the utter uniqueness of every other person, love, sex, suffering, and death.

Because obscenity rejects each of these educational goals, it is an attack on civilization. By capitulating to obscenity, civilized society denies there is any difference between civilization and barbarism. It is reasonable to assume that a depraved moral outlook can translate into depraved conduct—i.e., more crime. . . .

Some secular psychologists recognize the damage pornography can do to society as a whole, in addition to its devastating impact on individuals. Dr. Blain E. McLaughlin, a Freudian psychiatrist and consultant to the U.S. Department of Justice, is an expert witness in obscenity cases. He has testified in more than 100 such cases. In an interview with a newspaper reporter, he had this to say about pornography's threat to civilization:

Pornography can have an influence on the general population. Pornography miseducates the public, reinforces abnormal sexual attitudes. We object to hard-core misidentification of sexual material—that's where the damage is, particularly because of the inexperience of the young.

Pornography is not sex—it is sick sexuality. There is the danger the pathologically inclined

> might substitute pornography for normal sex.
> The young (through pornography) are taught
> the wrong thing about sex. It is sexual
> miseducation. . . . When you're teaching
> something that's abnormal you're poisoning the
> educational water supply. And it tends to ruin
> a neighborhood.

He might have said, just as factually, that it tends to ruin a city, a country, a society—civilization itself.

Dr. Victor Cline, a clinical psychologist who did the psychological assessments on two survivors of the infamous Houston sex murders, gave a chilling report on the pernicious effects of pornography in testimony before a committee of the Texas state legislature in 1978.

He noted that many studies show empirically that when pornography spreads into a community unchallenged it brings a number of other social ills along with it. Prostitution, drugs, homosexuality, sex-related crimes such as rape and incest, and all manner of social problems seem to be pornography's fellow travelers. In support of this contention, Dr. Cline pointed to the well-documented case of New York City's Times Square. The same tendencies have been found in other places such as Copenhagen and Amsterdam.

First, he called attention to a plethora of "sex clinics" that have sprung up across the nation. These clinics use hard-core, erotic films as part of a therapy designed to treat sexual dysfunction. Using Pavlovian conditioning, these films are supposed to help in the correction of such sexual problems as impotence in men and frigidity in women. They are even said to be useful in changing sexual orientation—that is, changing a homosexual to a heterosexual. In some cases, these films are said to be successful in this type of therapy.

Dr. Cline states, "If people can be re-conditioned by these explicit films [for a good purpose]. . . , then one has to allow for the possibility of negative conditioning in teaching socially deviant sexual behavior by exposure to malignant kinds of pornographic films and erotic stimuli."

In other words, the psychologist is saying, if pornography can be used to teach one thing, it can be used to teach another. If it can change an undesirable sexual attitude to a desirable one, it can change a desirable sexual attitude to an undesirable one. That, he asserted, is precisely what happens when people expose themselves to pornographic materials.

Dr. Cline said: "We are all subject to the laws of learning. We are all affected by what we experience, and no man or woman is exempt.

"Pornography can get its corrupting venom into a person sometimes even when he or she is accidentally exposed to it," Dr. Cline said. "I don't care who you are," he said, "we are all vulnerable to this. I, myself, have to be extremely cautious about the kinds of things that I expose myself to, because of this high risk factor. Even though I have done research in the area (of pornography), I am very conscious of this and cannot be involved in any way with it."

The psychologist said he did not mean to imply that every person seeing a pornographic film or reading a pornographic book will be inspired to go out and commit the acts depicted. He did cite considerable evidence, however, that pornography has a cumulative effect on the minds of people who continually expose themselves to it. He gave this case history of one pornography victim:

> I had a patient—a couple—that I was seeing in marriage counselling. The husband had become addicted to viewing local sex films shown in "adult theaters." He had become what we call a voyeur. . . . [Voyeurism is a minor form of sexual deviation.] He was "turned on" sexually by watching other people performing sex acts.
>
> He now prefers to see . . . these films than to make love to his wife, who feels profoundly rejected and is chronically depressed. She happens to be a very attractive and affectionate woman. . . .
>
> As she put it to me, crying, "What does that two-dimensional woman on the screen have that I, his wife—a loving, affectionate person—can't give him?" Of course, she doesn't realize that, to some extent, he has re-channeled his sexual interest into watching others and fantasizing about the sexual activity, rather than to engage in it with a live sexual partner, his wife.

Dr. Cline offered another example of the insidious working of pornography to corrupt the mind and life of a "healthy" individual:

"In another case, treated by a colleague of mine, a thirty-year-old junior executive saw pornography which had repeated themes of sado-masochism and group sexual activity. [He became captivated by fantasies derived from this exposure.] This led to many problems in his marriage. He has asked his wife to play roles to this fantasy, which includes using whips and other kinds of things and having his wife participate in these activities."

The psychologist gave yet another example of how pornography can corrupt a mind, this one involving a professed Christian:

"A gentleman I treated—a man who has been very active in his church, has a family—had a problem with pedophilia, sexual attraction to girls of the ages of eleven to thirteen. As we explored his history and studied his past, we found that the conditioning could be traced to early pornography in his middle or early adolescence which included seeing explicit sexual themes introducing fantasies into his brain which resulted in deviant behavior. He is very concerned about what he is doing, but he compulsively acts out his behavior every once in a while. He has lost his 'free agency' of control."

This expert testimony, coupled with reports supplied daily by the news media, provides evidence enough that pornography constitutes a grave threat to society. Crime statistics support what Dr. Cline said concerning the relationship between pornography and criminality. Many such statistics are available, but in illustrating the point I will quote only one. In my home community, Fort Worth, Texas, reported incidences of rape have risen alongside the spread of pornography in the area. The rate of increase has reached a dramatic level—26 percent (from 252 to 319 in one recent year)—and the upward trend is continuing at a steeper pace.

However, crime statistics don't begin to reflect the extent of the damage pornography is doing to society. We may never know how many cases of child abuse, how many unhappy marriages, how many listless, unproductive lives might be traced to the insipient poisoning of pornography. But we do know that anything so diametrically opposed to God's truth and his precepts of dignity of the individual could not help but create havoc in any society it is able to permeate.

The greatest threat pornography poses to human society may be through the destructive force it unleashes against marriage and the home.

In Genesis 2, we are told that after creating man God saw that it was not good for man to be alone. So he created a suitable companion for him—a woman. That episode reveals that God's chief purpose for sex—for creating them male and female—was love and companionship.

God was able to see to the heart of man's need. Man's need wasn't sexual stimulation. It wasn't strange, erotic thrills. It wasn't instant gratification for his biological drives. God saw that man's real need was love and companionship. God said, "It is not good that man should be alone" (Gen. 2:18).

By depicting sex as merely a physical or mechanical activity engaged in for the thrill of it, instead of what God meant it to be—an expression of love and companionship—pornography attacks the spiritual basis of marriage. Men and women whose minds are affected by pornography inevitably bring its perverting and distorting concepts into their marriage relationships. There it ferments and produces its foul fruit—dissatisfaction, disillusionment, depravity, degeneracy.

Dr. Cline, the psychologist, says it is not unusual for those addicted to pornography to try to persuade their marriage partners to engage in bizarre sexual behavior with them. The result is inevitably trouble of one kind or another. If the marriage partner submits, he or she may find the unnatural behavior degrading, if not painful. This can lead to marital problems and divorce. If the marriage partner refuses to participate in the suggested behavior, this also can produce discord and, ultimately, disintegration of the marriage.

Even if the pornographic exposure never leads to suggestions of imitative behavior in the marriage, however, it can still cause problems. It can interfere with the thought life and sexual attitudes of its victims in subtle ways that deprive them of fulfillment in their marriage relationships. Again, the result can be a broken marriage and a dissolved home.

Pornography is a weapon in the hands of the enemies of God. It strikes viciously at the love, purity, and respect God established as the basis for all human relationships, particularly that of marriage.

History has proven time and again that marriage and the home are the building blocks of society. By undermining these foundations, pornography works to weaken and destroy a nation. It may be that political enemies of the free nations have conspired to contaminate America and other Western countries with pornography, as some have suggested. But political conspiracy is hardly necessary as an explanation for the spread of pornography. Spiritual conspiracy, engineered by Satan and his minions, would suffice to explain it.

And, in the fallen sin-nature of man, the devil finds a willing accomplice. It provides the lust to be exploited and the greed that is only too eager to do the exploiting. We will see this in the next chapter, which deals with the pervasive and perverting qualities of pornography.

TWO

HOW PERVASIVE?

Few born-again Christians would deny that pornography presents a threat to the biblical values that have prevailed so long in America. However, some might underestimate the seriousness of the threat. Because they don't frequent the places where pornography is distributed, except perhaps by accident, they don't fully realize how pervasive a problem it has become. And, because they seldom observe its results, they don't comprehend what a perverting influence it wields in society.

Forbes, a magazine which describes itself as "a capitalist tool," published a nine-page report on pornography as an industry in one of its issues. The content of that report offers some insight into the scope of the pornography problem in America.

According to the *Forbes* report, the California Department of Justice estimated that, as of 1978, U.S. pornographers were doing a $4 billion business annually. That is equal to the combined volume done by the "conventional" movie and record industries. And, the article said, the actual sum of pornography sales may be twice that high.

Other facts revealed by the report were:

—The ten leading "skin" magazines gross $475 million a year.

—"Adult" film theaters total two million admissions a week and take in $365 million a year.

—Another $100 million in sales is recorded for sexual devices euphemistically called "marital aids."

These items account for a little less than $1 billion of the pornographic industry's annual gross. *Forbes* said that much of the remaining $3 billion in porn business is done "in the thousands of adult bookstores and peep shows around the country." The report said a Times Square store can easily gross $10,000 a day. Los Angeles stores take in $125 million a year, three times more than the retail sales of I. Magnin, one of the big retail chains in the area.

The porn business has become so lucrative that many "respectable" people are getting into it for the money they can earn. Bob Greene, whose column is syndicated by Field Newspapers, Inc., wrote recently about Joanna Farnsworth, a thirty-six-year-old mother of three who, he said, "has been president of her local PTA and a singer in her church choir." She has written seventy-six pornographic novels, Greene said, describing her work as the kind of "hard-core smut that has given pornography its bad name." Mrs. Farnsworth explained her career as a porn writer to Greene:

"It's a nasty way to make a living. But I'm divorced, and I have to raise the kids. I was writing poetry before, but that didn't pay very well. This pays $300 to $400 per book, and I turn out two or three books a month. If I'm going well, I can do a book in five days. I aim for 20 or 30 pages of double-spaced copy a day."

Many other people who "need the money" are writing pornographic material, taking pornographic pictures, producing pornographic films, or promoting, distributing, and selling pornographic materials of one kind or another. I have seen no estimates of the number of people who may be involved in this degenerative industry, but the annual volume of business suggests that the number is alarmingly large.

Thus, by material standards of measurement, pornography is big business in America. And, because it is bad business, it is also a big problem.

In many of America's large cities, the magnitude of the pornography business has become odiously evident. Most Americans know how Times Square, one of the traditional fun spots in the country, has been taken over by the peepshows, skin flicks and hard-core bookstalls. A news service report from Houston, Texas, reveals that New York City is not the only victim of the smut trade.

The article tells how a Houston housewife was unable to sell her home because the porn dealers had converted the neighborhood into a sex strip. "I hate for anybody to even come to my house to visit," the woman was quoted as saying. "It was a nice neighborhood until they [the operators of sexually oriented businesses] moved in a couple of years ago," she said.

She and a number of her neighbors appeared before a committee of the Texas legislature to complain not only about the sex businesses but also about the drugs and other evils that came along with them.

Responsible adults in many communities have become alarmed about the corrupting influence these pornographic invasions can have on a neighborhood, especially on the young. But the pornography peddlers are not stopping at the neighborhood level. They are intent upon pushing their product into the homes, into the living rooms and bedrooms of America.

For some time, they have been trying to work through the mails. This avenue has been restricted by laws that curtail the type of material that can be mailed to a residential address. The effectiveness of these laws depends largely on the alertness and responsibility of the parents in the home, however. And an increasing number of parents seem to care little what their children see or receive through the mail.

The don't-care attitude of parents is opening another door through which pornography can enter the home. The vehicle in this case is the home videotape machine, a new consumer product with much potential for good.

Like most things capable of being used for good, though, the videotape system is being made a tool for evil. According to some reports, almost half of the cartridges being bought for home videotape viewing are pornographic.

Apparently, pornography is not the only skill of those who deal in this disgusting business. They seem quite proficient at fraud, too. Many of the pornographic tapes allegedly feature famous actresses who are said to have made the films when they were struggling starlets. The actresses deny they are the women in the films, and the quality of the movies is reported to be so poor that reliable identification of the characters would be impossible. More than likely, most critics conclude, the characters in the film are not who they are said to be, and the viewer is a victim of fraud.

The greatest fraud perpetrated through videotape porn, however, is its misrepresentation of sex. And since this form of pornography exists in the home, many children will inevitably be exposed to it and have their attitudes influenced by it. Ultimately, the defrauded ones will be the home, which depends on a wholesome understanding of sex, and the nation, which depends on the strength of the home.

THREE

HOW PERVERTING?

Judges are getting tired of the war on pornography, a magazine article said, but not for the reason some might suspect. What dismays some judges is the sheer boredom of having to read all the dirty books that come to court in obscenity cases. "The characters are totally forgettable, and whole sections of the books can be interchanged among each other without disturbing the continuity of any of them," the article said.

A Freudian psychiatrist has sounded a similar theme. In a newspaper interview, he said: "Pornography wears you out after a while. There is a shock value to it, but it only lasts for about 10 seconds. It's hard to keep interested because it gets boring. How many poses of gyrating couples or groups can there be? I have seen two-hour movies without a human face in them. And because the shock value soon disappears, they are always inventing new things, like child pornography."

His last sentence points to the peril of dismissing pornography as harmless on grounds that it is boring to some people. It is extremely dangerous for the very reason that it does become boring. It pushes the thrill-seeker toward ever more bizarre erotic material in an effort to satisfy his unnatural appetite for sensual pleasure.

Dr. Victor Cline, the clinical psychologist quoted earlier, explained in his testimony before a Texas legislative committee how pornography works to drag its victims deeper and deeper into the jaws of degradation. He said:

> In treating a number of patients in my private practice who have become immersed in a pornographic milieu, I find four things occurring. . . .
>
> First, I find that there is an addiction to pornography. The individual, and it's almost always a male, gets "hooked" on the material and comes back again and again for more (in the same way that) one gets "hooked" on a powerful drug like heroin.
>
> Secondly, I find there is an escalation factor in which the person increasingly wants to see and be exposed to more and more deviant obscene material. In other words, it takes in time rougher, more deviant, more explicit material to give the person his "kicks."
>
> Thirdly, I find that eventually a desensitization occurs; that is, what was originally shocking, antisocial, distressing (even though still sexually stimulating), in time becomes acceptable. The person is no longer shocked or offended by the material. . . . He is able, in his own mind, to rationalize extremely deviant kinds of acts such as rape . . . brutal rape, injury to children [during] sexual activity. No longer does he become shocked or offended by this.
>
> Fourthly, what I find is that, eventually, the man urges his sex partner or his wife or even sometimes other members of the family to engage in such sexual activities, many of which are extremely deviant and anti-social. . . .

No one is more aware of the progression—"regression" might be a better word—followed by the porn addict than the people who provide him with the filthy "fixes" he seeks to maintain his habit. To keep degenerate junkies hooked, the porn pushers continually change their products, making them more and more deviant and bizarre. The trend is from explicit acts of normal sex, to deviant sex, to brutal sex and finally to cruel and inhumane acts that to the normal person might seem totally unrelated to sexual behavior.

Dr. Cline traces the "progression" of pornographic materials marketed across America.

> Originally, the pornography shown in major urban areas of the U.S. consisted of little more than . . . hour after hour of sex scenes showing normal, natural sex acts—nothing more. However, now, in order to attract new audiences, increasingly deviant material is being presented, which often includes children, rape, sado-masochism, group sex, as well as interpersonal violence associated with sexuality. A constant diet of these kinds of materials can and does affect a person's fantasy life, later his behavior and eventually even his most basic values."

Evidence abounds in support of Dr. Cline's findings concerning the addicting power of pornography, the escalating desire it excites in its victims, its desensitizing effects, and the tendency of the porn addict to act out the behavior he sees in the pornographic material.

Male readers of skin magazines have shown the effects of pornography on their minds by involving their wives and girl friends in producing pornographic material. One magazine claims to receive 65,000 pictures of nude wives and girl friends each year, many of them too lurid to be printed even in its filthy publication.

This alone demonstrates the perverting power of pornography. What could be more deviant or more defiant of God's plan for the husband-wife relationship than for a man to offer a nude photograph of his own wife for lustful strangers to leer at? A news report from Muskegon, Michigan, told of a woman having to be placed under psychiatric care after her estranged husband sold a nude snapshot of her to an international magazine and it was brought to her attention by her friends.

This was an extreme case that received public attention through the news media. But how many more women are being humiliated and degraded by husbands or boyfriends who have become sexual freaks as a result of pornography addiction? God's plan is for husbands to love their wives as Christ loved the church. Christ gave himself for the church that he might sanctify her and purify her (Eph. 5:24, 25), and that is how God commands husbands to love their wives. Pornography allows no room for that kind of love. It not only robs husbands and wives of the joys of true love but even deadens their ability to think of one another as persons, as individuals deserving consideration and respect.

Pornography attacks the home not only by perverting the husband-wife relationship but also by destroying the natural and God-given relationship between parents and children.

Dr. Cline's finding that the porn addict eventually tries to persuade someone to engage in deviant behavior with him deserves special attention. While the person approached usually is the porn addict's wife, Dr. Cline said it may be "other members of the family." More and more frequently, these "others" are the porn addict's own children.

One family counselor told a newspaper reporter that, based on reliable surveys, it is estimated incest occurs "in at least 5 to 15 percent of all families." Brother-sister relationships account for much of the incest, the counselor said, but father-daughter relationships also are commonly reported. The effects of these incestuous encounters with their fathers is devastating to little girls.

Almost invariably they [the girls] will have trouble establishing relationships with the opposite sex. They are confused about affection and sex, and often the only kind of affection they recognize is sex.

They have low self-esteem and a lot of guilt. They feel a lot of the responsibility for the incest, thinking, "If I'd been the right type of daughter, it wouldn't have happened."

Many times they are seduced and not forced [into incestuous relationships]. There is an emotional closeness which isn't available any other way. They feel angry and guilty on one hand and closeness on the other hand. There is a feeling of uniqueness—they feel they are the only ones it happens to. There is so much pain they believe they are the only ones with that experience.

The counselor said girls and women who have been involved in incest with their fathers often come for counseling for other problems, such as depression or anxiety, and the incest surfaces as the root of the problem. It is a characteristic of incest victims not to reach out for help, the counselor said, explaining:

"They are isolated people—emotionally and

otherwise. The father who commits incest has not developed the skills for establishing close relationships [of any kind] with people, not just sexual relationships. To get his needs for warmth and nurturing met, he marries and the marriage deteriorates. Then, because of the stress, he turns to the child in the family. . . ."

The sin of incest creates a chain reaction because, the counselor said, the child to which the father turns does not get her needs met. "And so the cycle goes on, generation after generation."

The counselor's observations concerning incest parallel what psychologist Cline said about pornography—that in the guise of being sexual it is actually antisexual. "Not only does it not promote healthy, good sexual relations, but it actually disturbs the relationship between men and women," Dr. Cline said.

Not every case of incest can be traced to the influence of pornography, but psychiatrists, psychologists, and social workers report that pornography has been a factor in many such cases.

The escalating aspect of pornography points to its godless nature and origin. The Apostle Paul describes the same degenerative pattern in detailing the course followed by society as a whole once it has turned its back on God. In Romans 1 (NASB), he identifies these descending moral stages:

1. They "suppress the truth in unrighteousness" (v. 18). Pornography suppresses, or shoves aside, the truth about sexuality as God intended it to be. In the place of the tender expression of love that God created and ordained, pornography substitutes a counterfeit in which sex becomes a heartless means of exploiting another person for self-gratification.

2. They dishonor their own bodies in unrestrained efforts to satisfy the insatiable lust for impurity that fills their hearts (vv. 24, 25). The pornographer depicts activities so dishonoring to the human body that decent people have been made ill by the sight of them.

3. They lose their God-given attraction for the opposite sex and begin to lust for persons of the same sex (vv. 26, 27). Pornography pictures and describes homosexual and lesbian behavior and has been proved a factor in the conversion of "straight" people to homosexuality.

4. They become filled with all manner of unrighteousness—not just sexual unrighteousness. Their lifestyles are characterized by greed, malice, envy, strife, deceit and even murder (v. 29). Pornography and its addicts have been known to display all of these characteristics. In fact, one student of pornography has posited that its ultimate goal is murder—not merely the destruction of the personality but of the total person, physically as well as psychologically.

5. They become "slanderers, haters of God, insolent, arrogant, boastful, inventors of evil, disobedient to parents" (v. 30). Pornography's captives have shown all of these odious traits.

6. They are "without understanding, untrustworthy, unloving, unmerciful" (v. 31). The addicts of pornography, and many of those engaged in the production and sale of it, exhibit a lack of understanding about the vital issues of life. They show an inability to distinguish between right and wrong. They often are heard to justify their evil activities on grounds that they help people overcome "sexual hang-ups" or enhance their sex lives. Much of what I

report in this book reveals the pornographer and his customers to be altogether untrustworthy, unloving, and unmerciful.

7. They not only practice utter unrighteousness but, although they know their actions are worthy of death, they urge others to do the same things and give them their hearty approval when they do (v. 32). There is ample evidence of this tendency among those who wallow in the filth of pornography.

The theme of much pornography graphically depicts its God-defying nature and its penchant to defile everything that is pure and decent. In one film the "plot" is reported to be a motorcycle gang's invasion of a Catholic church. The hoodlums brutally slay a priest and then rape several young girls who are participating in confirmation rites. Another film is about two girl scouts who, while selling cookies door-to-door, are lured into the home of a man. The girls are seduced and subjected to unnatural and extremely explicit sexual acts.

Some producers of pornography might scoff at the suggestion that they are urging people to act out the scenes they see in pornographic materials. But they cannot deny that they want more and more people to buy pornography, and that the evidence shows that as they do buy it many of them learn and practice what pornography preaches.

The consensus of evidence indicates that deviant sexual behavior is learned. Dr. Cline says: "There is no sexual deviation that I know of that is inherited. Every sexual deviation is learned in one way or another."

One way in which it is learned, he said, is through "conditioning."

If what psychologists report about the "sex

clinics" that use pornographic films in therapy is true, the effectiveness of pornography as a vehicle for conditioning has been proven.

Dr. Cline tells about a study that reveals how "conditioning" by pornography works. The study showed how it is possible to witness, live or on film, graphic sexual acts that stimulate recurring fantasies which become self-perpetuating. These fantasies, he says, become a powerful reinforcement leading to actual behavior—" . . . child molestation, rape, etc." Dr. Cline adds this chilling observation:

"In other words, it [pornography's conditioning power] leads to acted out deviant sexual behavior. In fact, this is how sexual deviation starts. . . . Any kind of sexual behavior can be acquired in this way, and these deviations are practically impossible to eliminate. Talk with an 'exhibitionist.' He can be from a high status in life or from any income level, and you'll find he has lost his 'free agency' in this area. Even though he is aware of the great risk involved, he still loses control and goes out and acts out this behavior, at great danger to himself, humiliation to his family, etc."

The psychologist notes that films such as the ones mentioned earlier, involving innocent young girls, could be extremely dangerous. They could "potentially condition some male viewers to fantasies and later behavior involving seductive sexual experiences with children," he said.

In discussing these horrible, satanic distortions of sexuality, it is important for us to remember that sex in itself is not dirty, frightening, or harmful. Sex is God's gift to men and women, and practiced as he intended it to be, sex becomes an important part of the foundation of marriage and the home. The great evil of pornography lies precisely in its design to spoil what God created and pronounced to be "very good" (Gen. 1:31).

Studies of the effects of pornography show that this healthy bond of love is subject, especially in males, to being twisted into a violent and irrational obsession. The sexual impulses God meant to be constructive in the husband-wife relationship can be warped into a destructive perversion.

Perhaps the most alarming finding of these studies is that it is not, as commonly assumed by decent people, merely the mentally deranged who fall victim to pornography's brain-warping effect. It can destroy the thought life of any man. It can undermine the sex life of any couple. Dr. Cline puts it this way:

"It makes no difference, I have found, what your intelligence or social status or position in life is. . . . We are all vulnerable and capable of doing injury."

He gives some examples:

—A forty-six-year-old deputy mayor of Los Angeles, a distinguished public servant, who was found guilty of committing a sex crime with a young girl. He had to resign his prestigious job and abandon his career. "There is almost no doubt at all that the [pornographic] material he saw on the screen helped stimulate him to the point where he lost control," Dr. Cline said.

—A Brownie girl scout in Atlanta, Georgia, brutally raped and murdered, the victim of a man who, the evidence suggested, had recently been exposed to pornography which not only helped to trigger the act but also planted in his mind some of the things he did to the girl.

—A man who spent one-and-a-half hours watching a hard-core pornographic movie in a North

Hollywood theater then, prompted in part by what he had seen, went out and raped the theater cashier.

In a study of rapists in Southern California, Dr. Michael Goldstein found that 57 percent of the study group of sex offenders admitted to actually trying out sexual activity they had seen during exposure to pornography. Of a group of molesters of children, 87 percent indicated that pornography had stimulated them to commit sexual acts with the children.

Hardly an edition of the daily news goes by without publicizing some outrageous example of deviant sexual behavior in the United States.

The federal government is still investigating what appears to be a nationwide child pornography and prostitution operation based in Chicago. *The Chicago Tribune* reported that key evidence in the case consists of between 50,000 and 100,000 pink file cards believed to list the ring's customers from coast to coast—along with their sexual preferences. Police seized the card file in the home of a paroled convict who had been sentenced to prison for molesting several boys. Believed to be the leader of the ring, the man was arrested on charges of contributing to the sexual delinquency of minors after two teenage boys said he photographed them in the nude and had sexual relations with them.

The case illustrates many of the evil aspects of pornography—its addictive power, its conditioning to deviant behavior, its desensitizing influence (making it possible for a man to exploit and abuse young children without a twinge of conscience), and its pervasiveness. Imagine, up to 100,000 customers for child prostitutes and pornography depicting sexual perversions involving children! And this was the volume of only one porn and prostitution business!

One report told of a thirty-two-year-old man assaulting and murdering a seventy-eight-year-old woman in her home. The assault was executed with a curtain rod.

A man was convicted in California for kidnapping and raping a fifteen-year-old girl. The charges included attempted murder in the first degree, mayhem, two counts of forcible oral copulation, sodomy, and kidnapping. The depth of the perversion involved is revealed in the reason behind the "mayhem" charge. The assailant, in the course of his fiendish attack, chopped off both of the girl's forearms!

One study of rape reveals the warped mentality of those committing a certain type of rape. This particular crime is called, in psychological circles, the "power rape." The power rapist seeks control of his victim through intimidation with a weapon, physical force or threat of bodily harm. The victim is usually overwhelmed, kidnapped, tied up or in some way rendered defenseless. The assault, say the scientists, is premeditated and preceded by an obsessional fantasy. In this fantasy, the victim may initially resist the attacker, but once overpowered, she submits gratefully to his sexual embrace.

I repeat, not all such atrocious acts as I have just described can be traced to the influence of pornography. But by more than mere coincidence, I am convinced, much pornography depicts equally violent and shocking themes, including some of the very conduct reported in the news stories.

This apparent tie between porn and violence could hardly be a surprise for those who have studied the philosophical and psychological bases for pornography. In at least one heinous sex crime, the Houston mass murder, there can be no doubt of the contributing role played by pornography.

In that case, twenty-seven young men were lured to the home of Dean Corll where they were subjected to deviant sex acts and then murdered. Dr. Cline, who did the psychological assessments on the two survivors of that sordid experience, reports they admitted pornography influenced their behavior. One of the two said he had gone out and sought pornographic material to discover new ways he could torment and injure people while having sex with them.

In his testimony before the Texas legislative committee, Dr. Cline gave this analysis of the Houston crimes:

> [They involved] two young teenage boys and an older homosexual, Dean Corll, who was in his early thirties. Corll took these two teenagers and seduced them sexually. Then, through powerful manipulation . . . , he got them to participate in the sexual murders of the young boys they would recruit. All three of these people were involved in pornography and were "turned on" sexually by a variety of stimuli. The problem in this situation was the desensitization effect. . . . After they had killed two or three people, of course always sexually molesting them, they reached the point of desensitization. . . . These murders didn't bother them any more. One of the boys said, "The first one was a little bit upsetting; from then on it was no problem at all. . . ."

Romans 1 links sexual perversion with all other forms of social deviance—uncontrollable, irrational violence, conspiracy, malice, and murder. The link seems to be holding in today's society. No doubt many—perhaps even most—homosexuals are quiet, law-abiding citizens (except that their homosexual conduct is a crime in many states). But, despite the disclaimers of some of their spokespersons, homosexuals seem to crop up in association with a curiously large number of criminal activities.

A study of personality traits of homosexuals by one researcher may offer an explanation for this phenomenon. The results indicated that homosexuals, as a group, suffer more than the general population from masochistic provocation (desiring to be hurt or abused), defensive malice, depression, and guilt feelings.

A prison chaplain who spent much time with homosexuals in his ministry has theorized that the homosexuals' unnatural sex thoughts, actions, and emotions directly affect their glands and disturb the normal hormonal balance of the human body, upsetting the mechanism that keeps the emotions in equilibrium. This may account for some of the apparent association of homosexuality with other perverted behavior. Robert Betts of the Copley News Service noted, in an article on May 2, 1969, that in Nazi Germany elite members of the SS were introduced to abnormal sexual activities as part of the conditioning process to brutalize them.

In their most recent report, William H. Masters and Virginia Johnson, reputed to be the nation's premier experts in sexual behavior, note that homosexual fantasies about forced sex are more violent and sadistic than those among heterosexuals. If that is so, it adds to the evidence of an association between homosexuality and violence. Given the fact that homosexual behavior is learned and that pornography has been proved an effective teacher, a link also can be suspected between much homosexuality and pornography. This is not to suggest that pornography is the cause of homosexuality, but there is evidence that it can contribute to the development of homosexual orientation and behavior. Pornography also is used as an instrument by some homosexuals to recruit persons for their perverted pleasures.

The most sensational case of this sort was the Chicago mass murders. In that case, thirty-three boys and young men were homosexually assaulted and killed, then buried in the crawlway under the suspected murderer's home or thrown into a river. The alleged killer, who posed as an upstanding citizen, used his personal charm, part-time jobs, and other devices to lure his victims.

But among his most effective tools were pornographic movies.

FOUR

THE BATTLE FOR THE MIND

The Bible says that when men stubbornly refuse to acknowledge God as God, he gives them over to a depraved mind. They become so immersed in evil thoughts and schemes designed to fulfill their lusts that they lose all ability to distinguish right from wrong. They become desensitized to perverted and violent behavior that they once found shocking. It no longer upsets them to commit disgustingly deviant acts, to use other people in gratifying their unnatural cravings or even to injure or kill them. That is what it means to be given over to a depraved mind.

Recent developments in the field of psychology and sex behavior research illustrate how depraved mentality feeds on itself like a cancerous growth, spreading its lethal toxin throughout the social system.

Early in this century Sigmund Freud, the father of psychoanalysis, wrote that most men are driven to debase their sex partners. Until recently, most psychologists and psychiatrists have been unwilling to accept Freud's suggestion that sexual relations involve a degree of hostility. Now some of them are reporting increased evidence of links between sex and aggression.

Psychologist C. A. Tripp, for instance, has asserted that conflict is important to satisfactory sexual relations for both men and women. Without it, happy marriages eventually sour, he has said. Masters and Johnson, the sex researchers cited earlier, say their studies indicate that violent sexual fantasies are surprisingly common.

Los Angeles psychoanalyst Robert J. Stoller has made an even stronger statement regarding the alleged link between sex and violence. In his book, *Sexual Excitement,* he said: "It is hostility—the desire, overt or hidden, to harm another person—that generates and enhances sexual excitement. The absence of hostility leads to indifference and boredom."

Stoller comments in another book, titled *Perversion,* that "we [normal people] try to make the outlandish folk function as scapegoats for the rest of us, but anyone—not just analysts—who collects erotic thoughts knows that many citizens, avowedly heterosexual, conspicuously normal . . . are also filled with hatred and wishes, if not plans, to harm others."

In making our own evaluations of the findings of these researchers, Bible-believing Christians should keep two questions in mind.

First, from whom are the researchers getting the bulk of their data? Beginning with Freud and leading down to the present day, they are getting most of it from people who are having problems in their sex lives. These are the people who ultimately are driven by their internal misery, or perhaps their overt criminality, to the psychoanalyst's couch. Much of the remainder of the researchers' information comes from people who do not believe in God or, if they do, are not letting him control their minds and their lifestyles. They are abnormal in their thinking and behavior.

Anyone who does not follow God's pattern for living is abnormal, because God's design for life is the only right and normal design, so the researcher gets an unbalanced view. Seldom, I would suspect, does the psychoanalyst or psychotherapist interview a born-again, Spirit-filled Christian. Rarely does he even see a person who, though not a Christian, adheres to Christian principles of decency and morality. He sees for the most part people who reject God and Christian principles, and his findings reflect their abnormal sexual orientation.

In the case of the famous Masters and Johnson studies, for example, much of the data is supplied by men and women, many of them prostitutes, who allow themselves to be wired with electrodes and observed as they engage in sexual activities in a laboratory. Are these laboratory "guinea pigs" sexually "normal" people?

Considering the sources of their information—mostly people with sexual problems or those willing to walk in off the street and give sexual performances under a microscope, so to speak—just how valid are the findings of these widely publicized studies of sexual behavior?

My own conclusions are that most of these studies do not depict true sexuality. They do not show normal sex—sex as God designed it, sex that is a tender, private expression of love between a man and a woman who are totally and eternally committed to each other.

I am convinced that the studies reveal the distorted fantasies and lusts of depraved minds. Minds that have rejected God and his righteousness. Minds that have been given over to "degrading passions," to doing "those things which are not proper," filled with "envy, murder, strife, deceit, malice" (Rom. 1:26, 29, NASB).

Yet, because they are presented as evidence of "normal" thought and behavior, these findings contribute to the same false picture that pornography paints. They foster the belief that the abnormal is normal, that what God and even the human conscience say is wrong and depraved is really right and natural.

In so doing, the so-called scientific studies help pave the way for widespread acceptance of the sick and misleading messages of pornography. These messages include the idea that there is a natural link between sex and aggression and that violence—even that forceful enough to cause bodily harm or death—is a means of enhancing the sex thrill.

Is it any wonder that America's institutions, built on the foundations of Christian morality, are beginning to crumble?

Whether we realize it or not, a great war is continually being waged for control of the minds of man.

The mind is a channel for thoughts and ideas and an activating mechanism that commands the body to behave according to the mind's directions. But every mind has a master. A mind either serves the true God or it serves some false deity. "No man can serve two masters," Jesus said (Matt. 6:24).

So when a mind is set to reject God's control, it is automatically handed over to the control of some other power. Those who defend pornography as an instrument of intellectual and sexual freedom are deceiving themselves and trying to deceive others. Paul said, "Know ye not, that to whom ye yield yourselves servants to obey, his servants ye are . . . whether of sin unto death, or of obedience unto righteousness?" (Rom. 6:16). Pornography is not an instrument of freedom. Rather, it is an instrument of enslavement to depraved lifestyles that lead to death for the individual and destruction for society.

God strives to reach and draw minds to him through his Word, his Holy Spirit and the revelation of his Son. Jesus Christ is the light, the truth, whom God has sent into the world. But men, in their natural state, reject the light because it condemns the things they do for pleasure. ". . . men loved darkness rather than light, because their deeds were evil" (John 3:19).

Writing to Christians in the early church, Paul repeatedly emphasized the vital necessity for believers to give God control of their minds and let him supply the thoughts and ideas determining their attitudes and behavior.

In Romans 12:2, he said we are to be "transformed by the renewing of your mind." Christians should be different creatures from what they were before they received Christ (2 Cor. 5:17). They should embrace a different set of values. Their lives should exhibit different attitudes and different behavior patterns. To be "transformed" in this manner, however, Paul says there must be a renewing of your minds. The verb is in passive voice. We cannot renew our own minds. God must do the renewing. But he will do it only when we submit it to him for renewal, only as we "present our bodies [to him] a living sacrifice" (Rom. 12:1). By refusing to yield our minds to God, we accept the alternative to being transformed. We allow ourselves to "be conformed to this world." Again, the verb is passive. Being conformed is not something we do, but something we let the world do to us. When people reject God's renewing, in the belief they are gaining freedom, they are accepting the world's conforming action, whether they know it or not.

When a person becomes a Christian, Paul says, he should put away the old life and "be renewed in the spirit of your mind" and put on the new life, "which after God is created in righteousness and true holiness" (Eph. 4:23, 24).

The *New American Standard Bible* lends an interesting insight with its translation of verse 22. It says the old life, or "old self," is "being corrupted in accordance with the lusts of deceit."

Thus, Paul's warnings to Christians concerning the battle for the mind are fully warranted. The battle continues after we accept Christ. It may be even more fierce than before. The "old self" is still "being corrupted" by the lusts and deceits of this world. If we fail to "put off" this old self and, by the renewing of our mind, put on the new self given us in Christ Jesus, we will continue to let the world corrupt and conform us. We will never be useful instruments in God's hands.

Paul offers some valuable instructions as to how we can allow God to renew our minds, so that they do not fall captive to the controlling influences of the world.

In Colossians 3:1,2, he says: "If ye then be risen with Christ, seek those things which are above, where Christ sitteth on the right hand of God. Set your affection [mind] on things above, not on things on the earth." This entails changing our motivations and goals from what they were when we were unrepentant sinners. Then we sought after the things of the earth. Now we are to seek the things of heaven, the things that are of God. Then our minds dwelled continually on the things of earth—material possessions and sensual pleasures. Now we are to set our minds on things above, on God's thoughts and purposes for our lives.

Christians also have a responsibility to help each other keep their minds focused on spiritual things, Paul says. The *New American Standard Bible* translates his instructions in these words: "Let the word of Christ richly dwell within you, with all wisdom teaching and admonishing one another with psalms and hymns and spiritual songs, singing with thankfulness in your hearts to God" (Col. 3:16). We are not only to let the word of Christ saturate our own minds. We are also to teach and admonish one another in the Word, as expressed in the gentle, loving phrases of the psalms and hymns and spiritual songs.

While people don't control their own minds (they either let God control them or they let the powers of this world control them), Christians can decide what force they will surrender their minds to. By an act of the will, and by a discipline exercised by the Holy Spirit, they can choose what fills their minds.

Paul said: "Finally, brethren, whatsoever things are true [real], whatsoever things are honest, whatsoever things are just, whatsoever things are pure, whatsoever things are lovely, whatsoever things are of good report; if there be any virtue, and if there be any praise, think on these things" (Phil. 4:8).

Just how serious is this struggle for control of the mind? How important is it for Christians to follow Paul's warnings and advice about being renewed in their minds and keeping their minds in the controlling hands of God?

In summing up his testimony regarding the corrupting power of pornography, psychologist Cline said that "a powerful kind of link exists . . . between pornography and actual, real life behavior." Referring to addiction, escalation, desensitization, and imitation of pornography in behavior, he asked: "Where does this all start?"

His sobering answer: "It starts way back with a person who [at some time] is accidentally exposed to things like this [pornographic material]. They see pornography which 'models' deviant sexual activity which, at the same time, 'turns them on' sexually, [and that begins] a 'conditioning effect.' "

Christians must guard their minds against anything that might divert their attention from God's way and start their thought life hurtling down such a pathway to destruction.

The warning is not intended to strike fear in the hearts of believers. It is true that "greater is he that is in you, than he that is in the world" (1 John 4:4). But God's own counsel is that we would be wise to "abstain from every appearance of evil" (1 Thess. 5:22).

That counsel from the Word of God raises a question this discussion has not yet touched upon: What constitutes pornography? What types of material should Christians avoid because of its salacious and addictive sensual power? What is this mind-polluting matter that can spread depravity like an insidious poison through the arteries of society?

Until now, we have focused on some of the more advanced stages of the escalation that Dr. Cline identified in pornographic material—the progression from "natural sex" presented explicitly to unnatural and even bizarre sexual behavior. But "the other end of the scale" deserves equal attention.

This is where the devil uses some of his cleverest tactics to lure the unwary into his lascivious lair. Risqué humor, lewd suggestion, erotic nudity—these are identifying characteristics of the bait Satan uses to arouse interest in his inventory of more overt instruments of moral destruction.

These baiting devices fit into a category defined by author Susan Jacoby as "socially acceptable pornography . . . subtle things people don't think of as pornography." She mentioned, as illustrations, certain television programs and magazines that subtly associate sex with violence.

I like the term "socially acceptable," because it spotlights the escalatory aspects of pornography as clearly as any concept I have encountered. Plainly, what is "socially acceptable" today would have been shocking twenty years ago. People would have been outraged then by the movie marquees, magazine covers, and other displays that openly flaunt lewdness and depravity. Now such things stir little protest. They have become "acceptable" to an alarming number of people.

Hugh Hefner, publisher of *Playboy* magazine, boasts of being one of the engineers of this acceptance. In the spring of 1979 a TV special celebrating Playboy's 25th anniversary was aired by 200 affiliates of the American Broadcasting Company. It included film clips, photos, and graphics to illustrate the revolutionary changes occurring in the sexual, social, and cultural aspects of American life during the quarter-century of Playboy's existence. It also featured scenes of Playboy "bunnies" and women who had modeled for sensuous centerfold photos. Interviewed prior to the telecast, Hefner told a reporter that only the "liberalized atmosphere" in

America enabled the program to be aired. Then he claimed credit for having helped create such an atmosphere. He said:

"Playboy has been around a full generation, so a new generation has grown up in a different, more unrestricted environment. Playboy has had a significant influence in those social changes, but at the same time has reflected the change going on around it. We are now living in a climate very close to what Playboy was espousing."

Hugh Hefner is right. Playboy established a trend in American thought patterns. Because it was successful, other publications copied it, or tried to go it one better. Thus, the Playboy philosophy, which depicts women as playthings and men as animalistic exploiters, permeated our culture. It had a "conditioning" effect. By making this distortion of sexuality widely "acceptable," Playboy helped open the floodgates for a torrent of desensitizing smut and sado-masochistic sewage to inundate the country.

Just as marijuana can lead to LSD, then to cocaine, heroin, and other "hard" drugs, so *Playboy* and similar magazines can plant in the mind a craving for hard-core pornography. Once "hooked," an individual can be lured from one degree of depravity to another until his or her own life is a shambles, marriages and families are destroyed, and other people's minds are contaminated.

When this process occurs on a massive scale, as is now happening in the United States, an entire society can be undermined. History reveals that sexual deviation and licentiousness, the stock in trade of pornography, have played a major role in the collapse of past civilizations. Will America be the next to fall?

If not, it will be only because Christians awake from their apathy, shore up their own mental defenses against "socially acceptable" pornography, and begin to exert their influence to protect their neighbors from the hard-core pornographer's pernicious plundering.

FIVE

THE RIGHTS OF THE DECENT

Having established that pornography is an evil and a threat to individuals and society, we face two critical questions. First, would it be in keeping with the philosophical precepts of man as a free moral agent and with the legal structures of the U.S. Constitution for Christians to use legal an political action to combat pornography? Second, assuming that the first question receives an affirmative answer, just what can be done to dam the flow of pornography?

Constitutional lawyer William A. Stanmeyer, quoted earlier concerning the nature of pornography, has made one of the clearest and most forceful statements I have ever seen regarding the legal and philosophical grounds for opposing pornography. Here are excerpts from his article in *The National Observer*, May 16, 1977:

> *Pornography exploits. Pornography is exploitation. Pornography teaches exploitation. Yet we have otherwise serious lawyers and writers urging that society have no laws to protect its citizens from the harm that a vast majority of citizens correctly perceive will flow from the pornographic flood. Presumably this defense of moral pollution stems from misunderstanding what pornography is, or blindness to the harm it does, or mistake as to the impact control will have on freedom of speech, or confusion as to law's legitimate role in protecting public morality.*

The public wants the law to restrain pornography. Most "intellectuals" do not. The purpose of this article is to remind the intellectuals why the public is right . . . .

In defining obscenity, the Supreme Court has said the basic guidelines are "(a) whether the average person, applying contemporary community standards, would find that the work, taken as a whole, appeals to the prurient interest; (b) whether the work depicts or describes, in a patently offensive way, sexual conduct specifically defined by the applicable state law; and (c) whether the work, taken as a whole, lacks serious literary, artistic, political, or scientific value." This is a definition, a workable one, as precise as such phrases as "due process," "the public interest," or "reasonable man"—standards the law uses daily.

Some writers insist such a definition will bring repression of Shakespeare or the Bible. This view suggests there is no difference between art and trash—and it says a good deal about their critical faculties and disdain for the public's common sense, not to mention their unfamiliarity with Shakespeare and the Bible . . . .

The Founding Fathers were not absolutists. They upheld legal sanctions against libel, indecent speech and conduct, profanity, and other abuses of free speech. They knew the difference between liberty and license. They knew freedom can be abused. They did not deem free speech to be solely a question of "rights" of the speaker. They also considered the purpose of speech, which was to foster the politically and morally Good Society.

It is not always easy to decide what conduct is "reasonable," what process is "due," what material is pornographic. But we must try. What must be balanced is not merely a publisher's asserted "rights" against a prosecutor's zeal, but also the harm to society from a few unwarranted obscenity convictions against the harm to society if every newsstand, TV screen, and even schoolbook panders a thousand pictures of perversion.

The absolutists say we cannot draw any line anywhere. This is patent nonsense. In a democracy, why should the minority who cannot distinguish between art and trash dictate the education—through magazines, television, and schoolbooks—of the children of the majority, who can tell the difference?

To say the law has no business promoting morality is to exhibit amazing ignorance of Anglo-American history. Nearly every branch of law assumes the existence of a standard of moral good and evil. Besides physical crimes such as murder and theft, the law proscribes "sharp" business practices, "unfair" political campaigning, racial discrimination . . . .

Society is more than an aggregate of individuals. Besides the pornographer's private "right," there is a public right to a decent social environment. As a parent of four little children, I have a constitutional right—recognized by the Supreme Court since 1925—to train my children to their higher obligations. To rear decent children requires that public entertainments—magazines, movies, TV, etc.—not be utterly indecent. The pornographer arrogates the "right" to teach my children to be indecent. Why should a few pornographers dictate the sociomoral environment of the children of millions of parents?

The law guides future generations as they grow into its precursive patterns. . . . To remove all legal control of pornography is to teach the young that their elders do not know right from wrong; that we do not care how our young entertain—that is, educate—themselves; that civilization and barbarism are the same. . . .

To the absurd assertion that laws proscribing the raunchiest of sex magazines will lead to censorship of Time and bonfires of National Geographic, I answer: This didn't happen in the past, when there was more censorship. The Supreme Court would not permit it. The alternative of saying "anything goes" is far more likely to lead to schoolgate bookstores glutted with picture books of homosexual rape and child torture.

Some say, "The best way to deal with pornography is to let it run its course; once sated, people will get bored with it." This is somewhat like saying the best way to deal with the filth in Lake Erie is to let Lake Erie fill up till it can't take any more. Why should parents have to let their children's moral environment get so corrupt that by comparison Sodom and Gomorrah resemble a Trappist monastery?

> The salient issue is, May we draw a legal line
> somewhere? Or must we draw no lines? Must
> we tolerate everything, no matter how de-
> praved, how sick? The public's answer is, We
> will draw a line, because we have the right to
> rear decent children in a decent society; and
> children or no, decent adults have a right to a
> decent society. And the public is right.

Sentiment for taking legal steps to stem the tide of
pornography runs high not only among conservative
Christians and attorneys but among political liberals
as well. Katherine Hepburn, an actress who rose to
stardom before movies acquired "R" and "X" rat-
ings to denote the degree of obscenity they con-
tained, had long been considered a liberal on most
public issues. When she appeared on the television
program "60 Minutes" in 1979, however, she let the
world know she believes in a measure of censorship.
She said:

"We're looking at filth and I'm disgusted with the
movies. Disgusted, because they're kidding themselves into saying it's [the obscenity] a sort of intellectual pastime. Bunk! It's 42nd Street filth, and the
critics have lost their minds. And how can it be
stopped? They say, 'Oh, no censorship. No, no.
Freedom of the press!' [But] they've got to do something. I mean you've got to have censorship. Life is
full of censorship."

Miss Hepburn, let me emphasize, was talking
about the "socially acceptable pornography" presented in the movies shown in theaters throughout
America. If some form of censorship is justified in
the case of this type of material, then surely there is

justification for legal action against the far more toxic hard-core pornography that saturates many of our neighborhoods.

Because of the demeaning, dehumanizing way it depicts women and girls, some women's lib activists have become ardent proponents of antipornography legislation. This seems to be the one issue that unites feminists and those who oppose the women's lib movement which, in some respects, is itself contrary to God's ideal design for womanhood.

Not all feminists agree that pornography should be fought with legal weapons, however. Susan Jacoby, the author who deplores the groundswell of "socially acceptable pornography," is one who firmly disagrees.

In her newspaper interview, she contended that outlawing pornography would only force it underground. It would not eliminate the "brutish subculture" that causes pornography to thrive, she argued.

"Feminists who want to censor what they regard as harmful pornography have essentially the same motivation as other would-be censors," she said. "They want to use the power of the state to accomplish what they have been unable to achieve in the marketplace of ideas and images. The impulse to censor places no faith in the possibilities of democratic persuasion."

While it's true that no antipornography law would eliminate the "brutish subculture," I believe Jacoby's conclusions are invalid. Because we cannot eliminate the brute is no reason to abandon our efforts to bind and control him. We may not be able to rid ourselves of the brute, but we can prevent his mounting a frontal attack against our children, our marriages, our homes, and our neighborhoods. The brute has ever been among us, but we have not in the past allowed him to run amok in our streets and leave his smutty footprints in our living rooms, and we don't have to allow him to do so now.

One flaw in Jacoby's argument lies in her failure to recognize the spiritual essence of the pornography issue. Pornography is an instrument of Satan that wields a sinister influence over the fallen nature of man. Once that is recognized, it should be obvious that it's rubbish to talk about combating pornography in terms of "the marketplace of ideas." Pornography is not an idea. It's a psychological drug. It can't be fought with ideas any more than heroin and cocaine can be fought with ideas. It must be combated with laws that protect the vulnerable minds of children—and adults—from its furtive powers.

No one knows better than I the importance of our First Amendment freedoms. I have waged a personal struggle for freedom of speech and freedom of religion, risking my evangelistic ministry to defend every citizen's right to hear and be heard. I believe these are God-given rights, and that they are monumentally important to the propagation of the gospel message.

In the midst of my most fervent pronouncements in behalf of free speech, however, I have acknowledged that freedom of speech is not an absolute freedom. As the lawyer quoted earlier said, the Founding Fathers themselves didn't envision it as an absolute freedom. Many kinds of speech already have been prohibited by law—slander, incitement to riot, and sedition, to name a few.

Also on that list of prohibited kinds of speech, though some seem to have forgotten, is obscenity. Laws have been passed in most states and communities prohibiting obscenity, and the constitutionality of many of these laws has been upheld by the courts.

It is not, as some insist, a violation of either the Constitution or America's democratic traditions to outlaw pornography. On the contrary, it is a legitimate and—I'm convinced, an absolutely essential—approach to defending and preserving America's traditional freedoms. Why? Because those freedoms are founded on a concept of man as a being of worth and dignity, not as an animal or an object to be exploited by animals, and it's at that priceless concept that pornography aims its most vicious assaults. If we let decency be destroyed, freedom will die at its side.

In upholding the constitutionality of certain obscenity laws, the U.S. Supreme Court issued the definitions of the term "obscenity" given earlier in the William A. Stanmeyer quotation. The court's guidelines leave the public defenseless against a loathsome mass of objectionable material, but they allow plenty of room for effective legal action against the most outrageous forms of pornography.

First, the court has said, a ruling that an item is obscene would depend on "whether the average person, applying contemporary community standards, would find that the work, taken as a whole, appeals to the prurient interest."

This definition of obscenity allows for two things: It allows public standards of morality to be used in determining what is and is not obscene, and it allows the standards to differ from one community to the next.

Allowing public standards to settle the issue presents some dangers to the cause of combating pornography. It makes antipornography law vulnerable to the "conditioning" work of "socially acceptable pornography." This conditioning, as Hugh Hefner boasts, is capable of changing public standards so that what might be defined as obscene today, under the court's guidelines, might not be considered obscene five years from now. Permitting different standards for different communities further complicates the matter. Pornography distributors who operate nationwide are already contesting in court the constitutionality of the differing standards.

About those community standards, psychologist Cline said:

"I would go along with the suggestion of the Supreme Court that there can be communities where there is greater conservatism, other communities where there is greater liberalism, greater latitude. But, in the end, if we really believe in the notion of democracy, a community should be able to make those decisions themselves."

The point is that the decent people of every community should assert themselves and demand that community leaders adopt a set of workable antipornography laws that will hold up in court under the "community standard" guideline.

The next factor to be decided in obscenity cases, the Supreme Court has said, is "whether the work depicts or describes, in a patently offensive way, sexual conduct specifically defined by the applicable state law."

This definition presents some difficulties for antipornography law writers, too. "Patently offensive" is a term that seems almost tailored as a loophole for the pornography to wriggle through. Even the term "sexual conduct" requires precise definition, and some definitions would be narrow enough to let an appalling amount of pornographic filth ooze past the legal barrier to contaminate a community.

However, it is not impossible to write a law that will snare the most offensive pornography and, at the same time, stand up in court.

Finally, the Supreme Court has said obscenity is determined on the basis of "whether the work, taken as a whole, lacks serious literary, artistic, political, or scientific value." This sounds like a guaranteed loophole that would make it impossible to get an obscenity conviction for any offense short of open sexual violence. Fortunately, however, much of the hard-core filth peddled by the pornographer is of such miserable literary and artistic quality that it is obviously of no value for anything but to pollute the mind and corrupt the community. As a result, much of the material that would be found to "appeal to the prurient interest" and to depict or describe sexual conduct in a "patently offensive" way would also be adjudged totally lacking in literary, artistic, political, or scientific value.

Once workable and constitutionally valid laws are enacted, pornography fighters face another problem: Getting the laws enforced.

Psychologist Cline said in testifying in support of strong antipornography laws that "the main issue is effective prosecution." He noted that in some areas where there are laws on the books to control child pornography, local prosecutors show little interest in prosecuting offenders.

One reason for their lethargy toward obscenity lawbreakers is that the prosecutors see pornography as a "victimless crime." Dr. Cline protested that attitude.

"This is totally untrue," he said. "There are all kinds of victims." His testimony, and the reports of many other experts in the field, support that statement. The victims include, first, the pornography viewer himself, then those whom he enlists to act out his unnatural fantasies, then the community as a whole and, finally, the nation.

The fact that some prosecutors refuse to prosecute pornographers indicates that the mere enactment of laws is not enough to win the battle against obscenity. Something more is required.

In this regard, Christians and others striving for a decent society could learn much from the radical pressure groups that have sprung up across the country in recent years. With some of their causes most of us would vehemently disagree. But we must admit that their tactics have been effective.

The key to this effectiveness has been well-planned, well-organized political action. The militants get the attention of the news media with public announcements and well-timed marches, rallies, and protest actions. They write letters and place telephone calls to editors and to TV station officials and network executives. They stage demonstrations. They send delegations to present their views to city councils, governors, state representatives, and congressmen. They receive contributions to pay for advertisements and to hire skilled lobbyists to promote their causes.

Because some of the tactics these groups use are unethical, if not illegal, decent people would not want to copy everything they do. But decent people should become politically active. Some boast about our "silent majority." A "silent majority" is a stupid majority. It's a majority that will lose its rights because it won't fight for its rights. It's a majority that allows itself to be dictated to by militant minorities. I do not advocate the denial of rights to any minority. I am saying only that the majority of the American people still believe in biblical principles of decency, and it is time for that majority to lose its silence, find its voice, and take a stand for what it knows to be right.

Such activism goes against the grain of many decent citizens. We've been taught that it's a virtue to live quiet, peaceful lives and avoid strife, and that is true. But it is not necessary to be unruly or obnoxious to get a point across to people in government. In fact, it is a Christian duty to do so.

The least that decent citizens can do is organize themselves, go to public meetings where public officials meet and let their views be known at the policy-making levels of their communities. If that does not get results, it would not be wrong for decent people to picket offensive theaters or newsstands or even the offices of uncooperative public officials.

In the political arena, pressure is the name of the game. People in positions of public trust respond to pressure from the people. Pornography is almost out of hand in America today because the decent people of this country have applied too little pressure too spasmodically in defense of values they endorse. In many communities, the decent citizens have seldom spoken out against pornography; in some, not at all. Where they have spoken out, they have often lost heart at the first discouraging development and quit the field of battle without a fight.

If the decent people of America would only organize, speak up for what they believe, and stick to their guns when the going gets rough, they could win the war against pornography. Then they could save their country from the moral cesspool that has swallowed other great civilizations.

SIX

WHAT CAN BE DONE?

In its report to the Texas legislature in January 1979, the Texas house select committee on child pornography made thirty-nine proposals. One called for the death penalty for murder committed in connection with aggravated sexual abuse. The committee had been convinced by its investigation and the testimonies of expert witnesses that pornography was a threat demanding prompt and effective defensive action.

Unwittingly, perhaps, the report supported the message that Romans, chapter 1, speaks concerning sexual deviance—that it is associated with other evils which are characteristic of the sinful nature of fallen man. It stressed, for example, that child pornography is inseparable from the larger problem of sexual abuse of children.

The report said: "Many of the [pornographic] films show children obviously unwilling to participate, as they may be held down or pushed into action by other children or adults. . . . Much of the materials have clear themes of sado-masochism . . . . The dominant theme is that sexual abuse of children is enjoyable and socially sanctioned by the sexually 'liberated' members of society."

The committee's recommendations, therefore, ranged beyond the subject of pornography. In addition to making aggravated sexual abuse a capital offense, they included proposals for:

—A law making it a penitentiary offense for doctors and hospitals to fail to report cases of sexual abuse.

—A law requiring owners of "adult" bookstores, X-rated movie houses, modeling studios, and massage parlors to file affidavits of ownership with the state attorney general.

—A law allowing building owners to void leases when their property is used for purposes of obscenity.

—A requirement that persons selling or distributing obscene materials must keep confidential records of the names and addresses of persons from whom they obtain their material. The information could be disclosed only to law-enforcement officers.

—A law prohibiting open display of sexually explicit material in commercial establishments generally accessible to minors.

—An amendment to the Texas Penal Code making aggravated incest a felony offense.

—An addition to the code prescribing sentences of two to twenty years in prison for persons convicted of incest on the second offense.

—Legislation establishing a procedure for making background investigations of previous sex offenses and requiring employers to use the procedure when hiring persons whose jobs would include working with children.

—Statutes requiring special training for police officers and school counselors in dealing with sex abuse cases, including interrogation and investigation methods.

—Laws allowing emergency removal of children from homes in which there is reasonable cause to suspect children are being sexually abused.

—A sentence of up to one year in jail for harboring runaway minors.

—The establishment of state facilities to provide temporary shelter and care for runaway minors.

The legislature to which these proposals were presented considered six of the eleven recommendations that dealt directly with pornography. Of these six, two were passed and signed into law by Governor William Clements. At this writing, supporters of strong antipornography legislation feel that the governor will urge consideration of three other measures during the next session, since he has expressed personal interest in seeing the proposals become law.

The Texas story proves that even a handful of concerned Christians and other decent citizens can deliver telling blows against obscenity when they make up their minds to stand and fight.

The bills introduced in the Texas legislature were modeled after legislation that has passed court tests for constitutionality in other states. As a guide for citizens seeking antipornography legislation in other states, here is the wording of four of the most important of the Texas bills, the first two of which are now law in the state:

HOUSE BILL NO. 1741, relating to the definition of obscene and to the elements of and penalty for the offense of obscenity:

SECTION 1. Section 43.21. DEFINITIONS.

(a) In this subchapter:
    (1) "Obscene" means material or a performance that:
        (A) the average person, applying contem-

porary community standards, would find that taken as a whole appeals to the prurient interest in sex;

(B) depicts or describes:

    (i) patently offensive representations or descriptions of ultimate sexual acts, normal or perverted, actual or simulated, including sexual intercourse, sodomy, and sexual bestiality; or

    (ii) patently offensive representations or descriptions of masturbation, excretory functions, sadism, masochism, lewd exhibition of the genitals, the male or female genitals in a state of sexual stimulation or arousal, covered male genitals in a discernible turgid state or a device designed and marketed as useful primarily for stimulation of the human genital organs; and

(C) taken as a whole, lacks serious literary, artistic, political, and scientific value.

(2) "Material" means anything tangible that is capable of being used or adapted to arouse interest, whether through the medium of reading, observation, sound, or in any other manner, but does not include an actual three-dimensional obscene device.

(3) "Performance" means a play, motion picture, dance, or other exhibition performed before an audience.

(4) "Patently offensive" means so offensive on its face as to affront current community standards of decency.

(5) "Promote" means to manufacture, issue, sell, give, provide, lend, mail, deliver, transfer, transmit, publish, distribute, circulate, disseminate, present, exhibit, or advertise, or to offer or agree to do the same.

(6) "Wholesale promote" means to manufacture, issue, sell, provide, mail, deliver, transfer, transmit, publish, distribute, circulate, disseminate, or to offer or agree to do the same for purpose of resale.

(7) "Obscene device" means a device, including a dildo or artificial vagina, designed or marketed as useful primarily for the stimulation of human genital organs.

(b) If any of the depictions or descriptions of sexual conduct described in this section are declared by a court of competent jurisdiction to be unlawfully included herein, this declaration shall not invalidate this section as to other patently offensive conduct included herein.

SECTION 2. Section 43.23. OBSCENITY.

(a) A person commits an offense if, knowing its content and character, he wholesale promotes or possesses with intent to wholesale promote any obscene material or obscene device.

(b) An offense under Subsection (a) of this section is a felony of the third degree.

(c) A person commits an offense if, knowing its content and character, he:

(1) promotes, or possesses with intent to promote, any obscene material or obscene device; or

(2) produces, presents, or directs an obscene performance or participates in a portion thereof that is obscene or that contributes to its obscenity.

(d) An offense under Subsection (c) of this section is a Class A misdemeanor.

(e) A person who promotes or wholesale promotes obscene material or an obscene device or possesses the same with intent to promote or wholesale promote it in the course of his business is presumed to do so with knowledge of its content and character.

(f) A person who possesses six or more obscene devices or identical or similar obscene articles is presumed to possess them with intent to promote the same.

(g) This section does not apply to a person who possesses or distributes obscene material or obscene devices or participates in conduct otherwise prescribed by this section when the possession, participation, or conduct occurs in the course of law enforcement activities.

SECTION 3. If any portion of this Act is declared unlawful by a court of competent jurisdiction, this declaration does not invalidate any other portions of this Act.

HOUSE BILL NO. 1742, relating to the offense of disseminating harmful material to minors.

BE IT ENACTED BY THE LEGISLATURE OF THE STATE OF TEXAS:
SECTION 1. Section 43.24. DISSEMINATING HARMFUL MATERIAL TO MINORS.

(a) For the purposes of this section:
  (1) "Minor" means any person who has not attained his 18th birthday.
  (2) "Nudity" means the showing of the human male or female genitals, pubic area, or buttocks with less than a fully opaque covering or the showing of the female breast with less than a fully opaque covering of any portion thereof below the top of the nipple or the depiction of covered male genitals in a discernible turgid state.
  (3) "Sexual conduct" means an act of masturbation, homosexuality, sexual intercourse, or physical contact with a person's clothed or unclothed genitals, pubic area, buttocks, or, if the person is a female, breast.
  (4) "Sexual excitement" means the condition of human male or female genitals when in a state of sexual stimulation or arousal.
  (5) "Sado-masochistic abuse" means flagellation or torture by or upon a person who is nude or clad in undergarments or in a revealing costume or the condition of being fettered, bound, or otherwise physically restrained on the part of one who is nude or so clothed.
  (6) "Harmful to minors" means that quality of any description or representation, in whatever form, of nudity, sexual conduct, sexual excitement, or sado-masochistic abuse, when it:
    (A) considered as a whole appeals to the prurient interest in sex of minors; and
    (B) is patently offensive to prevailing stand-

ards in the adult community as a whole with respect to what is suitable material for minors; and

(C) considered as a whole, lacks serious literary, artistic, political, and scientific value for minors.

(b) A person is guilty of disseminating harmful material to minors when:

(1) with knowledge of its character and content, he sells or loans to a minor for monetary consideration:

(A) any picture, photograph, drawing, sculpture, motion picture, film or similar visual representation or image of a person or portion of the human body which depicts nudity, sexual conduct, or sado-masochistic abuse and which is harmful to minors; or

(B) any book, pamphlet, magazine, printed matter, however reproduced, or sound recording which contains any matter enumerated in Paragraph (a) hereof, or explicit and detailed verbal descriptions or narrative accounts of sexual excitement, sexual conduct, or sado-masochistic abuse and which, taken as a whole, is harmful to minors; or

(2) knowing the character and content of a motion picture, show, or other presentation which, in whole or in part, depicts nudity, sexual conduct, or sado-masochistic abuse and which is harmful to minors, he:

(A) exhibits such motion picture, show, or other presentation to a minor for a monetary consideration; or

    (B) sells to a minor an admission ticket or pass to premises whereon there is exhibited or to be exhibited such motion picture, show, or other presentation; or

    (C) admits a minor for a monetary consideration to premises whereon there is exhibited or to be exhibited such motion picture, show, or other presentation.

(c) A person who engages in the conduct described in Subsection (a) of this section is presumed to do so with knowledge of the character and content of the material sold or loaned or the motion picture, show, or presentation exhibited or to be exhibited.

(d) In any prosecution for disseminating harmful material to minors, it is an affirmative defense that:

    (1) the defendant had a reasonable cause to believe that the minor involved had attained the age of 18; or

    (2) such minor exhibited to the defendant a draft card, driver's license, birth certificate, or other official or apparently official document purporting to establish that such minor had attained the age of 18 years.

(e) An offense under this section is a Class A misdemeanor.

HOUSE BILL NO. 1742, relating to a sexual performance by a child.

BE IT ENACTED BY THE LEGISLATURE OF THE STATE OF TEXAS:

SECTION 1. Section 43.25. SEXUAL PERFORMANCE BY A CHILD.

(a) In this section:

(1) "Sexual performance" means any performance or part thereof that includes sexual conduct by a child younger than 17 years of age.

(2) "Obscene sexual performance" means any performance that includes sexual conduct by a child younger than 17 years of age; any material that is obscene, as that term is defined by Section 43.21 of this code.

(3) "Sexual conduct" means actual or simulated sexual intercourse, deviate sexual intercourse, sexual bestiality, masturbation, sado-masochistic abuse, or lewd exhibition of the genitals.

(4) "Performance" means any play, motion picture, photograph, dance, or other visual representation that is exhibited before an audience.

(5) "Promote" means to procure, manufacture, issue, sell, give, provide, lend, mail, deliver, transfer, transmit, publish, distribute, circulate, disseminate, present, exhibit, or advertise or to offer or agree to do any of the above.

(6) "Simulated" means the explicit depiction of sexual conduct that creates the appearance of actual sexual conduct and during which the persons engaging in the conduct exhibit any uncovered portion of the breasts, genitals, or buttocks.

(7) "Deviate sexual intercourse" has the mean-

ing defined by Section 43.01 of this [Texas penal] code.

(8) "Sado-masochistic abuse" has the meaning defined by Section 43.24 of this [Texas penal] code.

(b) A person commits an offense if, knowing the character and content thereof, he employs, authorizes, or induces a child younger than 17 years of age to engage in a sexual performance. A parent or legal guardian or custodian of a child younger than 17 years of age commits an offense if he consents to the participation by the child in a sexual performance.

(c) An offense under Subsection (b) of this section is a felony of the second degree.

(d) A person commits an offense if, knowing the character and content of the material, he produces, directs, or promotes an obscene performance that includes sexual conduct by a child younger than 17 years of age.

(e) A person commits an offense if, knowing the character and content of the material, he produces, directs, or promotes a performance that includes sexual conduct by a child younger than 17 years of age.

(f) An offense under Subsection (d) or (e) of this section is a felony of the third degree.

(g) It is an affirmative defense to a prosecution under this section that the defendant, in good faith, reasonably believed that the person who engaged in the sexual conduct was 17 years of age or older.

(h) When it becomes necessary for the purposes of this section to determine whether a child who participated in sexual conduct was younger than 17 years of age, the court or jury may make this determination by any of the following methods:

(1) personal inspection of the child;
(2) inspection of the photograph or motion picture that shows the child engaging in the sexual performance;
(3) oral testimony by a witness to the sexual performance as to the age of the child based on the child's appearance at the time;
(4) expert medical testimony based on the appearance of the child engaging in the sexual performance; or
(5) any other method authorized by law or by the rules of evidence at common law.

HOUSE BILL NO. 1744, prohibiting the display of material harmful to minors in places frequented by minors.

SECTION 1. Section 43.26. INDECENT DISPLAYS IN PLACES FREQUENTED BY MINORS.
Exhibition to Minors of Indecent Publications, Pictures, or Articles.

(a) Every person who shall willfully or knowingly display at newsstands or any other business establishment frequented by minors under the age of eighteen (18) years, or where said minors are or may be invited as part of the general public, any motion picture or any still picture or photograph, or any book, pocketbook, pamphlet, or magazine, the cover or content of which is harmful to minors as that term is defined in Section 43.23 of this section commits an offense under this subsection.

(b) "Offense" in this section is a Class A misdemeanor.

SEVEN

THE ANSWER: REPENTANCE

In discussing legal steps Christians can take to hinder the spread of pornography, I do not imply that legal action is the solution to the problem. Pornography is a spiritual problem, not a legal one. Solving it calls for spiritual action. Legal action is totally inept when it comes to changing men's hearts and lives.

Legal action applied to pornography is analogous to first aid and the quarantines used in fighting a scarlet fever epidemic. The emergency medical measures won't cure the disease. They will only relieve some of the symptoms and curtail the rapid spread of the infection. By the same token, legal action cannot and will not heal the land of pornography. Though urgently important for what it can do in reducing the number of young people and adults contaminated by pornography's moral bacteria, legal action alone is not the answer to the pornography peril.

Romans, chapter 1, where we found the source of the pornography problem, also gives the solution. The passage says God gave men over to the reprobate mental condition that breeds pornography because:

—They refused to honor God as God, after God, through nature, had clearly revealed himself to them (vv. 20, 21).

—They exchanged the glory of the incorruptible

God for the image of an idol—the likeness of a bird, animal, snake, or man (v. 23).

—They exchanged God's truth for a lie and worshiped and served the creature rather than the Creator (v. 25).

—They refused to let their minds accept any thought or knowledge of God—utterly rejecting him (v. 28).

Pornography will be eradicated only when all of these attitudes and conditions are reversed, when:

—Men honor God as God, the sovereign God of love and forgiveness he has revealed himself to be.

—Men stop worshiping the false gods of this world—sin, pleasure, material things, and man himself—and worship the true God in "spirit and in truth" (John 4:23).

—Men forsake the lies they have allowed to deceive and seduce them and embrace God's truth, his holy Word.

When will this come about? Only when men repent, when they turn from their wickedness and call on the name of the Lord for forgiveness and salvation (Rom. 10:13). In Romans 2:4 (NASB), Paul reveals that this is God's purpose in dealing lovingly and patiently with sinful man: "Or do you think lightly of the riches of His kindness and forbearance and patience, not knowing that the kindness of God leads you to repentance?"

The wrath of God is revealed against all ungodliness and unrighteousness (Rom. 1:18), yet with kindness he leads the ungodly and unrighteous toward repentance. What a portrait of the matchless character of God! His wrath is upon ungodliness, but his mercy is upon the ungodly. He hates sin, but he loves the sinner.

This is the portrait we Bible-believing Christians must present to a lost and dying America if we are ever to see victory over pornography and the pantheon of evils it represents.

To beat pornography, we must not only pass and enforce laws that keep it out of the hands and minds of as many people as possible. We must also evangelize America. We must issue to this pleasure-loving, sin-captivated country a dynamic call to repentance—one that warns of God's wrath and proclaims his love.

If we present God's message of repentance and salvation clearly, convictingly, and convincingly, we can rely on the Holy Spirit to take his Word and do miraculous things with it. He can use it to cleanse, to transform, to impart eternal life.

God's Word is alive and powerful and sharper than a two-edged sword (Heb. 4:12). His Word will settle for nothing less than total victory in the battle for the minds of men.